Self Discipline Bundle

Self Discipline
Mental Toughness
&
Declutter Your Mind

By Martin Brandt

Self-Discipline

Mental Toughness

A Guide to Developing Your Grit and Increasing Your Productivity

Contents

Introduction

Congratulations on downloading your personal copy of *Self-Discipline and Mental Toughness: A Guide to Developing Your Grit and Increasing Your Productivity*. Thank you for doing so.

Self-discipline is a useful, important life skill necessary for successful people. Regardless of the area of life you're setting goals in, this skill will be essential. Although most people already know that it's important, there aren't many who actually take proactive steps to build and strengthen it in themselves.

The Misconception About Self-Discipline

There's a common belief about self-discipline being restrictive, tough, harsh, or limiting, but this is far from true. Self-discipline is about inner strength, knowing yourself, and having control. This valuable trait will allow you to follow through on your decisions, stick to your path, and accomplish amazing feats in life.

What Can This Trait Give You?

You will overcome laziness and procrastination, beat addictions, and radiate a strong sense of will. This book will give you the tools you need to build up a powerful sense of self-discipline, the fuel for your greatest desires. As you can see, you have nothing to lose other than some bad habits. So, if you're ready to change your life for the better, let's get to it. Thank you for choosing this book!

Chapter 1: Success, Motivation, and Choices

Success is something all of us crave, whether it's an ideal of how we want to look, how much money we'll earn, or even the type of family we'll eventually have. The idea of success almost seems, to many of us, like an elusive secret. We glorify the concept, place those who have success on a pedestal, and separate ourselves from it. But the truth is, success isn't a secret. If this is true, what is success? It's a *process*.

The Success Process

Success is not something you suddenly achieve one day; it's an attitude, a way of thinking, and a path to living. The subject that you want to gain self-discipline in will be highly personal for you, but there are some general guidelines that can help you along the way. How can you begin the process of success?

- **Define What Success Means to You:** Take some time to really think about this. What is the most important thing in the world to you? Who do you want to reach with your message? What does the ultimate vision of success look like for you? How will you know when you've gotten there? As soon as you have defined success for yourself, you'll be able to get on the path towards it.

- **Know Your Vision is Possible:** You won't be able to work towards your goal if you don't already believe in your heart it can happen for you. Once you've figured out what you desire, seek out other people who have already achieved this goal (either in person, in books, or online). This will inspire you and give you proof that your goal is possible!

- **Act No Matter What:** If you're going to wait around for the perfect time to act, you'll be waiting forever. You cannot depend on always feeling motivated to do something, even when it's something you deeply care about. Force yourself to take action, even on days that you're feeling lazy, and it will seriously pay off.

- **Try to Help Others:** Humans are social beings. We need connection. Providing and giving value to those around you will help you build stronger social ties that you can fall back on during hard times. Helping other people can also inspire us to stay on our personal path toward success. Instead of asking what you can get from any social interaction you're having, ask yourself what you can give. Success is not something selfish, but something only meaningful when it's shared.

The Truth About Motivation

How does motivation work? Oftentimes, this word brings thoughts of bonuses at work, material gains, or extra vacation. But the reality is, motivation is something more elusive than that. It's highly personal and, at times, not even reliable.

Deep, Intrinsic Motivation

If you aren't truly motivated to do a task, intrinsically (meaning you love doing it for its own sake), you probably won't do it. If you're only motivated by external awards, you likely won't stick to your goal.

Take the example of wanting to lose weight. Telling yourself you'll look much better may work for the first week in terms of getting you to the gym, but eventually, you will probably stop going. Reminding yourself that you want a longer life and that you deserve to feel great from the inside out, on the other hand, can be an intrinsic, meaningful source of motivation.

When and Why Motivation Doesn't Work

Sometimes, motivation just isn't effective. No matter how good our intentions are, all it takes is a different mood to slip up on our goals. Motivation can be a fleeting, changing state. This is why you can set your alarm at night, feeling motivated to arise at 6 in the morning and have a super productive day, only to groan and hit snooze when it goes off. For this reason, self-discipline is a far more reliable system than motivation.

You Have a Choice in Life

We have all been around people who seem to lose their minds when something stressful happens, completely shutting down and giving up. They act as though their states of being are out of their control, essentially forfeiting their own choice in the matter. But the truth is that though we can't always control stressful events in life, we can control how we react to them.

An event outside of you can only cause you to stress out if you make the choice to do so. I understand that when you're in the midst of a chaotic situation, your reaction feels like anything but a choice. But the fact is that stress is something we all go through in life. What differs is how we handle it and the best way to control how we handle it is through self-discipline. If you don't have a strong enough desire to learn how to handle stress in the right way, you won't do it. It's a decision.

Stress is constantly around us, but it doesn't become a part of you until you accept and internalize it. Everyone engages in stressed-out behavior every so often, but it doesn't have to be a habit. Here are the steps to control your reactions:

- **Notice them:** When an event pops up that makes you veer off course (whether it's giving up on your goal of losing weight and deciding to eat donuts or procrastinating on that test you're supposed to be studying for), notice it. What are the triggers that throw you off?

- **Record them:** The next step will be to write these triggers down along with the results that came from them. Now, these may not be nice to look at, but a truly self-disciplined person isn't afraid to view their faults. Only when you know what they are can you control and improve them.

- **Tiny Steps:** Now that you're fully aware of your weaknesses, it's time to make small changes toward shifting them. If you know, for example, that walking through the mall and smelling popcorn triggers you to want to give up on your healthy eating plan, stay away from the mall. If you tend to get angry whenever a certain relative calls, do some deep breathing exercises before you talk to them. These small shifts end up leading to big changes over time.

Chapter 2: Your Purpose and Positivity

Most people have no idea what they would like to do with their life. Some assume that it will eventually become clear to them as they get older, once they complete school, or once they're married. But the truth is that you may still have no clue, even after going through these big changes. Part of the difficulty with this question is the idea of "purpose" in life.

Many of us have a ton of baggage attached to this idea. We may believe that it's such a huge deal, or that without it, we're doomed to live a life of misery. Needless to say, this puts a bit too much pressure on the quest to find our life purpose. Try to approach the situation with a fresh perspective and an attitude of curiosity.

Questions for Finding Your Purpose

Finding your purpose should be an interesting, fun process and not something you dread or feel is an obligation. Feel free to mix and match these questions, or even add some of your own.

1. What Would You Do if Money Were No Object?

How would you spend your life if you already had all of your financial concerns covered? Perhaps you'd spend your days painting, helping other people through volunteer work, or golfing with your friends. Whatever this passion is, it's time to dedicate more of your life to it. It may become your life purpose, or it may just give you an outlet for relaxation and happiness. Either way is conducive to finding out what your purpose in life is.

2. Can You Handle Sacrifice for Your Dream?

The fact is that everything worthwhile in life involves sacrifice and comes at a cost. How much sacrifice can you deal with to reach your goal? Knowing the answer to this question will allow you to figure out how realistic one pursuit is in comparison with another. Here are some examples of sacrifices you may have to deal with if you pursue a specific path:

- If you want to be an entrepreneur, are you ready to face rejection time and time again?

- Do you want to be a writer without ever facing critique?

- Are you ready to give hours and hours of your day to your interest?

If these negative potential outcomes are enough to turn you away from something, then the goal is not your true path.

3. What Did You Love as a Child?

Certain things never change in a person. Oftentimes, what your favorite pastime was as a child can tell you a lot about what your life purpose could be now. For instance, maybe you loved to write stories as a kid and spent days doing it for the sheer joy and immersion it brought you. Odds are, whatever this interest was for you as a kid, you don't do nearly as much anymore. This could be because we've become self-conscious about our interest or that we only think things are worthwhile if they bring financial gain.

One of your first steps for reconnecting with your life purpose should be revisiting whatever it was your childhood self loved to spend hours doing. As a kid, do you think you would have stopped doing something just because you didn't think it was profitable or good enough? No, you would have done what you loved just because you loved it. Reconnect with that part of you.

4. When Do You Forget Time Exists?

Everyone has had an experience of the flow state, that state of mind that is so immersive that you forget to eat dinner. Maybe you get so immersed in coding that you don't leave your apartment for an entire day, which could be a big clue as to what your life purpose could be. Even an activity that is not typically thought of as "productive" such as gaming, could give you a hint as to what's important to you.

- **The Qualities Behind the Activity:** Taking the example of gaming, if you spend all day immersed in this activity, it could point to several traits or interests in you. You could thrive on a competitive atmosphere, for goal-setting, or general improvement in life conditions.

- **Applying those Qualities:** When you can apply the obsession you feel for self-competition and improvement to your passion or business, this will take you very far. For you, this could mean efficient organization, teaching, fixing problems, or something related to your social life. Whatever the case, make sure you are looking at the principles behind the activities to find what it is that makes it so addictive and compelling to you. These principles can be applied in other areas, too.

5. Being Okay with Vulnerability

When you're new to something, or rather inexperienced, you are probably going to be clueless at first. That's just the way it goes. And to be bad at something means you might end up embarrassing yourself and feeling vulnerable, probably over and over again. It's completely normal for people to try to avoid embarrassment, because it doesn't feel very good. But if everyone were to avoid the potential of doing something embarrassing, they would never reach new heights!

- **Acceptance:** You have to teach yourself to be okay with being vulnerable. At this moment, there's probably something you'd love to be learning about or pursuing, but reasons behind why you don't. These reasons are likely something you repeat to yourself on a regular basis. Often, these reasons have to do with potential reactions of other people to what you might do. Do you worry about being judged by your peers if you fail? Do you worry about your parents not accepting your new path? Then you're focusing on the wrong factors.

Accepting the possibility that others may not agree with your path and that it matters enough to you to stick with is the key here. Everything great on this planet is unconventional, unique, and to some people, shocking. So, you have to go against what others think to do anything amazing. This can be very frightening due to the fear of looking foolish or getting embarrassed. But what is the price to pay for ignoring your inner calling? Is it worth it to suppress yourself just to avoid a bit of embarrassment or scorn?

- **Seeing Your Newbie Status as a Strength:** A lot of times, experts or people who are very experienced in a certain field get stuck in concepts and don't know where to go. They find it hard to think creatively. For this reason, being new to something can actually be an advantage. You're seeing everything in the field with new eyes. This can apply to anything from business, to playing an instrument, to general self-improvement tasks. Someone who has a fresh, blank perspective can often see connections where others struggle.

6. Find Out How You Can Help

As I mentioned before, we are social beings and helping each other is important. Unless you live under a rock, you already know that the world has no shortage of current problems to focus on. What speaks most to you in this sea of issues? In order to be happy and satisfied in life, it's important to be a part of something bigger that benefits others. Here are some ideas for getting involved:

- **Helping the Homeless:** Do you feel a tug on your heartstrings any time you see a homeless person on the street? Don't ignore this! That could mean that you would get a lot out of volunteering your time at a shelter or finding other ways to help your fellow humans in need.

- **Writing about Issues:** Our education system isn't very great, domestic violence is a problem, and mental healthcare could use some improvement. All of these are issues you could be helping to spread the word about. Do you have a blog or a writing talent? Start using it to get information about something you care about.

Find something to care about and put your energies into helping. This won't mean you'll fix the issue on your own, but you will feel that you've made a difference, however small. And feeling connected to something and knowing you're making small, positive changes can do wonders for your self-esteem and will likely get you a little closer to finding your true purpose in life.

7. What Do You Want to be Remembered For?

Imagine that you just got a cancer diagnosis and know that you'll die within half a year. Yes, I know, it's not fun to think about dying and can be a scary thought. But this can give you many practical benefits. One of them is that it helps you discern what matters most to you in your life from what is pure, useless distraction. A lot of people wouldn't know how to answer this question, so if you have a little difficulty thinking of something on the spot, don't worry. Give it some thought before you find the answer. Here are other related questions to ponder:

- **What Will You Leave Behind?** How will
  others remember you once you leave this
  earth? Will it be mostly positive things or
  negative things? What can you do to make sure
  that you're remembered in a positive light
  when you leave this earth? If you can't think of
  anything but people saying impressive stuff
  about what you owned when you were alive,
  you probably aren't digging deep enough.

- **What are Your Values?** If you're having
  trouble deciding how you want people to
  remember you, it could be that you aren't sure
  what your values are or what matters most to
  you in life. This leaves you open to the danger
  of taking on the priorities of other people and
  allowing them to direct your life instead of you.
  This path can never lead to true happiness or

fulfilling relationships.

- **The Writing Test:** If you *still* don't know
what your values or purpose are, it's time to do
the writing test to get a little deeper. Get a piece
of paper (or an empty text document on your
computer, though actually writing with a pen
feels more personal) and write at the top "What
am I on this earth for?" Does this sound
dramatic? Good! Now just start writing. At
first, you may find that it's hard to know what
to say but keep going. Keep digging and
questioning until the words start flowing
naturally. This should give you some clarity.

Figuring out what your purpose is means finding out
what cause or goal you can be a part of that is larger
than you or the people around you. It's not about

earning $50,000 more per year or finally dating that specific person; it's bigger than that. How would your time be best spent? How can you make it more meaningful? If nothing comes to mind, you need to get out there and experiment more to find it. And that brings me to something else that will help you immensely along the way...

The Power of Positivity

Positive thinking is a bit of a buzzword these days, but what does it really mean? Although it's a no-brainer that most of us want to be more positive than negative, it's also a term that is so widely used it's lost a bit of its original meaning. But research is starting to reveal that it's about more than being upbeat and in a good, happy mood. Positive thinking can bring true value to your life, strengthen your self-discipline, and lead to all sorts of other useful skills in work and your personal life.

The results that positive thinking can have on your professional life, relationships, and even health is currently being observed by experts in psychology. Frederickson, a researcher of positive psychology at North Carolina university has found a few surprising new facts about how positive thinking can impact your skills in life. These useful bits of information can be applied practically to your life and self-discipline goals, no matter what they are specifically focused on. Here are some ideas from her research.

The Impact of Negativity

Science has known for a while that negative feelings prompt the brain to perform something specific.

When you encounter a potentially life-threatening situation, you get out of there as fast as you can. Suddenly, nothing else in your surroundings matters whatsoever in comparison. You will be focused completely on the threat, the state of mind created by the threat, and how to save yourself. Even if you do have a wide variety of choices available to you in the moment, your mind will narrow its focus and hone in on only one.

- **How This Developed:** In the early days of human development, this is a trait that saved our skins countless times, no doubt. Encountering a wild predator is one example of a scenario where that particular brain function would have come in handy. However, this is the modern world and that tendency can get in the way a lot of the time, rather than help us. Our brains are programmed to feel a threat (however insignificant in actuality) and turn the world off, limiting options and creating tunnel vision.

- **Examples of Negativity Tunnel Vision:** Imagine that you just got into an argument with your best friend and had to go to work immediately after. Odds are, in this situation, you would have a very hard time focusing on work and instead would be replaying the scenario over and over in your mind. Or what about those days where you know you have a task list a foot long and can't seem to prompt yourself to get started on any of the items on the list? In each scenario, your negative thoughts are closing you off to thinking creatively or seeing other choices.

The Impacts of Positivity

Now it's time to compare this with what happens in your brain when you are having positive thoughts.

- **The Experiment:** Fredrickson looked at the way positive emotions impacted the brain in an experiment where subjects were divided into groups and shown various video clips. The first group was shown images that prompted joyful feelings, while the second group looked at clips that made them feel content. A third group was the "neutral" group that was shown clips that had no emotion attached to them. Finally, there were two more groups shown feelings of fear and anger, respectively.

- **The Results:** After the groups were shown these clips, all of the participants were asked to envision a scenario that would prompt similar feelings and to record on a piece of paper how they would react. Each of them were given a sheet of paper with 20 sentences that began with "I would like to..." The group members that viewed images related to anger and fear recorded fewer responses. The group members who viewed content and joyful images listed many more actions they wanted to take compared to both the negative groups and the neutral group.

- **What Does This Show?** This experiment showed that when someone is feeling love, contentment, and joyful feelings, they will have more ideas and see more options. These were

some of the first scientific findings that showed
that positive thinking can broaden possibilities
and have a mind-opening impact. But that's
not all...

Positive Thinking and Other Skills

Positive thinking leads to even more advantages than
great feelings and more possibilities. Actually, the
greatest advantage that positive thinking brings is a
stronger ability to develop resources and build skills
that will help you later on in your life.

- **Unexpected Advantages:** Enjoyable habits
  can bring unexpected benefits. For instance, a
  kid who spends a lot of time outside with his
  friends, climbing trees, builds up the skills of
  athletic movement, social communication, and

creative reasoning. In this example, the positive feelings of joy and play help the child to develop skills that will help them in other areas of life later on. And these traits end up lasting a lot longer than the positive feelings that prompted them in the first place.

- **A Solid Foundation:** Later in the future, the positive foundation of social skills could lead to a prosperous career in team management. The joy that brought about the creation and exploration of new traits isn't there anymore, while the lasting impacts are. Positive feelings open you up to new possibilities, bringing you brand new resources and skills and giving more value to unrelated and often unexpected areas in life. This is the opposite of what negative feelings do. So, the next question is, how can

you be more positive in life to get these great
benefits?

How to Think More Positively

What actionable steps can you take to improve your skill of positive thinking? To start with, any action or activity that brings you feelings of love, contentment, or joy can help with this. You likely already have a few ideas in mind for that. It could be playing piano, hanging out with your spouse, or cooking. Here are some other general tasks to focus on that will bring you more positive emotions and benefits:

- **Positive Journaling:** Do you keep a journal? If not, it's time to start. Not only will this help you develop self-discipline by ensuring you stick with your goal of writing each day, but it can help you become more positive. In one study, a group of 90 participants were split into two different groups. One group was asked to write each day, for three days, on something intensely positive. The other group wrote on a neutral topic. A few months later, the participants who did positive journaling for three days had to visit the doctor less frequently and reported better moods and fewer sicknesses.

- **Make Time for Play:** Make some time in your life for playing. The average person schedules appointments, events, and meetings, so why not pencil in some playtime for yourself? Have you ever set aside an hour just for experimentation and exploration? Do you ever carve out some time specifically for fun and enjoyment? Happiness is at least as important as that work conference you have on your calendar, yet a lot of people don't act like this is true. Make time for this in your life and you will reap the wonderful benefits of positivity.

- **Gratitude Lists:** Looking for things to be grateful for is another great way to increase the amount of positivity present in your life. This can be done first thing in the morning or right before going to sleep (or if you really want to go above and beyond, both!) and can be done mentally or on paper. Make a list of what you are grateful for in that moment, no matter how seemingly small or big. Even if it's something like "The sun is shining today," that's a good start.

The Illusion of Putting Off Happiness

Most of us believe that success is what leads to happiness. And it's true that certain situations can bring you more joy. But having this perspective as a default might be preventing you from experiencing more happiness in your life. Do you often think that as soon as you make a specific change in your life you will finally be happy? Or maybe you think that once you buy a certain item, you'll feel joy again. How often does it actually happen? Chances are, you feel great for a short while and then it fades.

All of us are guilty of doing this to some degree. But the research on positivity we just covered should be enough to show you that happiness can be a great precursor for building the habits that will lead to success. So, happiness is not always the result of what you achieve but can also be the reason for your success. Happy people build new skills, gain new successes because of them, then feel even more joy, repeating this upward spiral ad infinitum.

Start making time to feel more positive emotions in life, by playing a sport, doing something creative, or just spending more time with your loved ones. This will lower your stress levels, make you smile, and even improve your self-discipline. Positive emotions and creative exploration open the door for reflection and growth in your life. The key to sticking with your chosen path is self-discipline, and the burden will feel much lighter with a positive approach.

Chapter 3: Dealing with Failure and Increasing Productivity

When it comes to the subject of failure, our own pride can be our worst enemy. Once events in life begin going the wrong way, we might go into survival mode, trying to maintain composure and possibly even lying to ourselves. But these common reactions, like clinging to what's changing, or denial, can ruin our ability to grow and adapt to changes in our lives. It can be extremely difficult to admit it to ourselves when we've messed up and try to fix it. Or we might hastily scramble to fix things, only to make them worse through a lack of forethought or careful planning.

Another common reaction to personal failure or mistakes is to lie to ourselves, pretend they didn't happen, or act like the mistake was a far lesser deal than it really was. We might be so nervous about what happened that we miss out on a real opportunity to fix it. So, all of this begs the question, how can we successfully adapt to change and deal with failure with grace?

How to Adapt Successfully

In our complicated world, it's necessary to keep an experimental, adaptive mentality and approach in order to reach success. We also need this attitude to develop a strong sense of self-discipline and excel at our goals. It's impossible to predict ahead of time whether the ideas we have or the risks we take will pay off once we launch them. Oftentimes, failure is inevitable, but there's good news! There is a way to fail in a productive manner. Here are the guidelines for failing productively:

1. Mix It Up

When you put all your eggs in one basket, a single failure can be very devastating. For this reason, among others, it's good to mix it up. Just as you should diversify your investments to avoid big losses, you should also have a wide variety of interests and plans in terms of business or your personal life. Even when it comes to hobbies, constantly looking for fresh ideas will help you see that a failure in one area isn't the end of the world, and you'll always have something else to fall back on.

2. Be Honest with Yourself

The next step for dealing with failure with poise is being completely honest with yourself about it when it does occur. Mistakes become much worse when you dwell on them or constantly beat yourself up over what happened. In order to rise above this common reaction, it's crucial to learn to recognize when you have failed. One way to recognize failure is to constantly ask for feedback from your peers. Asking someone you trust how you're doing and for honest critique can help you see a bit more clearly.

3. Get Rid of Attachments

This is hard when you're dealing with matters that are important to you, but handling failure in the right way calls for maintaining a healthy sense of non-attachment to outcomes. This doesn't mean you won't care; it just means that a single loss won't completely devastate you and throw your life off track. Stay adaptable, look for ways to grow, and always have a plan B.

4. Ask What You Can Learn

The best way to handle failure with ease and get more out of it is to ask yourself what you can learn from what happened. You may consider a low sales month at your job a failure, but dwelling on that and telling yourself you're no good isn't going to help. Instead, ask yourself what you did differently that may have contributed to the streak of low sales. Then ask yourself what you can do to make it better. Construct an action plan and you're already on your way to being productive with your failures!

Mastering the Art of Self-Discipline

Any master gets amazing at their art or trade by consistent practice, an attitude of devotion, and an openness to learning more. This is the approach required to become a master of self-discipline. Here are some practices that will help you gain an unshakeable and reliable sense of discipline that you can always fall back on no matter what happens.

Do It, Even When You Don't Feel Like It

Procrastination is an issue that most of us are familiar with. We usually procrastinate by telling ourselves that we simply don't feel like doing the task right now. It could be that the task is intimidating, confusing, or difficult in some way and makes us feel uncomfortable. This could lead you to seek a distracting or pleasant activity to occupy yourself with instead. The amazing thing is, in this mentality, we can find endless ways to occupy ourselves that help us avoid the task we know we should be doing.

Before you can start trimming your nails, checking Facebook, or watering your plants to avoid the task, begin the task immediately. Right when your mind starts to chime in and try to convince you to do something else, just do it anyway. Oftentimes, the fear of the task itself is far worse than the action itself.

Start Exercising Every Day

This is one of the greatest ways to build self-discipline because it's something that nearly every one of us has put off in one way or another. Exercise can feel hard when you aren't used to it, so we distract ourselves with something else, putting it off until "tomorrow" every day. But this can be seen as an ordinary part of maintaining your health, like brushing your teeth and eating. Show up to your exercise even when you're tired or don't feel like it. Odds are, you won't ever feel perfectly ready to do it, but you'll never regret a completed workout.

Learn to Recognize Real Hunger

Most people get anxious when they're hungry and reach for the closest thing to eat, even if it's junk, but the truth is that a little hunger isn't bad for you. In fact, many times, we use our hunger as a distraction tactic to avoid doing what we should be doing. So next time you feel the urge to reach for a bag of potato chips, analyze your hunger and see if it's real or an excuse to distract yourself. This is just an exercise that will show you that it's possible to be more conscious about your automatic decisions. This could also help you lose weight if that's a goal you have.

Face the Issue

Most of us avoid thinking about problems in our lives. Perhaps this is avoiding a financial problem, putting off a big project, or ignoring the fact that you need to get healthier. These realities can be hard to face because again, they make us uncomfortable and we'd rather ignore them. But try developing a new attitude towards problems in your life. Next time you notice an obstacle, see it as a different path. Acknowledge the path, find out as much as you can about it, and learn how to navigate. This will make you much stronger and more disciplined as a person.

Be Direct in Conversation

Make it a goal to have uncomfortable conversations. Most people avoid them because they can feel a little awkward or scary. But doing this just leads to problems including avoidance, resentment, and fights.

Instead of succumbing to the temptation of avoiding an awkward conversation at work or with your loved one, try to raise the issue in a compassionate, gentle and empathetic way. Ask them if you can talk, and then share your feelings. As long as you make sure you don't sound defensive and you do plenty of listening, it should go smoothly. Avoiding problems doesn't make them disappear, so get in the habit of facing your problems head on.

Look for the Good

Discipline is all about realizing that you don't need a huge, fancy award for everything you do. Getting things done is rewarding enough in itself. For example, you can learn how to relish going on a walk every morning instead of telling yourself that you can eat cake later if you do it. Or you can learn how to enjoy healthier foods instead of obsessively counting calories or dieting. Oftentimes, when you know how to look, the reward is in the new activity itself.

Remind Yourself of Intentions

One common challenge people undergo is staying true to their habit once the initial motivation wears off, as it inevitably does. It's not that hard to stick with something for a week, but it can get a little more challenging during the second or third week. Most people don't become masters of self-discipline because they quit before they get over the initial hump and don't give themselves enough time to establish momentum. Try committing to just one tiny habit for 60 days, even if it's only 5 to 10 minutes per day.

No matter what comes up, do this new activity each and every day at the same time and give yourself reminders on your phone or post-it notes around the house so you remember. Keep track of your progress on your calendar so you can see and celebrate your success. You can gradually add more and more positive, small habits. Before you know it, you will do these new habits without even giving them a second thought.

Using Self-Discipline to Become More Productive

There is no shortage of hacks, systems, articles, and tips on the internet that are designed to help with productivity and efficiency. But a lot of people who read blogs and books about productivity still find that they struggle to use the tools effectively. No matter how great the system is, an email organization tool won't do the work for you. No tricks or tips for becoming better at budgeting will think for you. The main issue for people who have a hard time with productivity is not an inability to learn new systems, but a lack of discipline.

The New Muscle

You can think of self-discipline as a new muscle that you haven't worked out before. At first, it's going to be a little tough, but it will get stronger the more you use it. Building your self-discipline from the point of view of productivity is being able to just do what you need to do. Depending on the field it pertains to, self-discipline can mean a variety of different things. If you're a musician, it can mean picking up your guitar every afternoon, even when you'd rather watch TV. If you're dedicated to learning a language, it means dedicating time each day to practicing.

Creating Results

But the most very helpful definition you can use for self-discipline is a tool to create results in your life. Everyone has ideas, but it's only the people who can get themselves to act that get any good results from them. Coming up with a system for organizing or processing email won't matter if you don't actually implement the new system when you have a chance.

Tips for Disciplined Productivity

But this knowledge is only the first step. Knowing something does not mean you will be productive. Only implementation can guarantee results. As stated, anyone can have a concept in their head, but it's only the people who know how to make themselves act on their ideas that will enjoy the success we all look up to and crave. Here are some tips for getting there.

1. Start Out Small

If you've never been able to bring about small ideas in your life, then it's going to be hard to make something huge happen immediately. Sure, it may work for someone every once in a while to attack a momentous goal and succeed at it right away, but for the rest of us, starting out small is going to be the best course of action. Let's return to the comparison of being disciplined to using a new muscle.

If you've never worked out your arms before, do you think you'd be able to lift an extremely heavy item?

No. And you won't be able to build a successful business or valuable, worthwhile habit overnight either. Here are some ideas for small changes you can begin implanting today:

- **Drinking More Water:** If you have a goal of losing weight, for example, it won't happen overnight. You are going to have junk food cravings for a while. But you can start with a small change like replacing your soda with lemon water or drinking your coffee without sugar. This can make a bigger difference in your weight than you realize.

- **Making Small Agreements:** If you're struggling with productivity or self-discipline, another good place to start is by making small appointments that you must stick to no matter what happens. This can be calling your mom every week, or something related to your business.

- **Unplug and Recharge:** More and more, people are starting to realize the benefit of turning off their computers and phones to allow their minds to rest. This small change can pave the way for a lot more productivity because you'll get the break you need. Try starting with just an hour of being phone-free per day, then work your way up.

Now, these changes may seem small or insignificant on their own, but they will add up to huge changes over time. And more importantly, you will learn that you have it in you to change any time you want to. With these small changes, your sense of self-discipline will slowly rise. Before you know it, you'll be tackling far bigger changes and feeling like a brand-new person!

2. Check Your Expectations

It would be a mistake to expect a weak muscle to be as strong as a muscle you're accustomed to using on a regular basis, and this also applies to your self-discipline muscle. Make sure that you aren't giving yourself unrealistic expectations or this will be much harder than it has to be.

3. Stay Accountable

When an individual has atrophied muscles and can no longer use them, they have to take intense therapy to rebuild strength. They must start out small and gradually increase the load until their muscles work again. This can also happen to your self-discipline, so you have to find a way to stay accountable. Whether this means signing up for a group or finding a partner who you can check in with, accountability is going to keep you on the right track towards your goals and keep you disciplined.

Try finding a person who is encouraging and helpful, who will be present in your daily life and wants to aid you in your goals. If you're trying to form a specific habit for professional reasons, then it can be a work colleague. But habits that have to do with your home life might be a little more complicated. If your goal is to quit smoking, for example, you may need a friend or relative to help you stay accountable. It's even better if this individual has the same goal as you, so you can lean on each other. If you don't know anyone in your life, check out groups online for support.

4. Give Yourself Challenges

For most people, routine can be the biggest enemy of success. This leads to sitting on the couch night after night or spending way too much time scrolling Facebook instead of pursuing worthwhile activities. But getting stuck in a rut like this will ensure that nothing new or exciting ever happens to us. And that's a serious issue. Contrary to popular belief, passion and enthusiasm are the byproducts of taking action, not the reasons for it.

- **Try New Things:** Figuring out what you care most about in life is going to take some time. And until you know, you'll probably be a pro at finding countless excuses for not pursuing more worthwhile activities. The fact is that no one knows how they will feel about something unless they try.

- **If TV Disappeared:** Ask yourself what you would spend your days doing if the television and Facebook suddenly disappeared and you had to leave your house each day to do something. Would you go back to school? Learn how to salsa dance? Take up snowboarding? It's time to stop putting off these activities and take action now.

Chapter 4: Meditation and Focus in Self-Discipline

The average person thinks that meditation is a mystical or difficult activity, but the truth is that it's very simple. Meditation can improve your self-discipline and focus in amazing ways. There are countless techniques for meditation, but it's best to start out with something simple at first. No one is good at meditation when they start out, but that's the point of practicing. You will soon learn as you continue practicing that you can stay with an activity, even if it seems hard.

Simple Beginner Meditation

You don't have to be a Buddhist to meditate. You can even start getting into the swing of it now. Throughout the day, start reminding yourself to focus on your breath and clear your mind. You can even set reminders on your phone. Go as long as you can focus on your breath and noticing every thought that comes up. Once you've done this for a few days, it's time to move onto sitting meditation:

1. **Sit Down:** The first step is to simply sit down. Some are flexible enough to sit cross-legged on the floor on a cushion comfortably, but most people will need to use a chair. If sitting in a chair with a straight back is uncomfortable for you, you can lie down, but try not to fall asleep.

2. **Keep Your Eyes Closed:** Now, gently close your eyes and keep them shut for the duration of this practice. Start breathing normally, but maybe a little deeper than you usually would. Try to breathe through the belly, allowing your abdomen to rise and fall, instead of through the

chest.

3. **Start with 2 Minutes:** When you first begin this practice, start with setting your alarm for only 2 minutes. This may sound like a pointless amount of time, but it's important to slowly ease into this. As you get comfortable with these 2-minute intervals, you can begin working your way up to longer periods.

Most people will get frustrated when they learn to meditate because they will find that their mind is extremely loud and active, trying to pull them away from sitting calmly. This is something you should expect and plan for, because it happens to everyone. This is normal and don't let it upset you. Just stay with it and be patient and it will get easier and easier. Soon, you may even find yourself looking forward to your meditation sessions when you notice how much calmer and more focused they make you.

There's No Such Thing as "Trying"

When we are "trying" to get something done, we may use limited time as an excuse not to complete anything. Perhaps it's a work project that you're trying to do, but you keep telling yourself that you only have a half hour of free time and that's not enough to get anything substantial done. Under this logic, watching TV or doing chores sounds like the more sensible thing to do. You tell yourself that you are "trying" to do something, when a lot of the time, that's simply not the case. You are either doing something or you aren't.

- **Avoidance:** Many times, trying is our way of choosing avoidance because we're afraid of something. Maybe we're afraid to change, afraid to disappoint our parents, or afraid of judgment from our peers for doing something different. Claiming to ourselves that we are trying is a convenient method for avoiding a commitment while pretending that you have committed. It's an avoidance tactic.

- **Change Your Language:** You must realize that the language of "trying" will make you fall short, because trying is not action. It's procrastination. Pay attention to the words you choose to use and keep in mind that you can either choose to do something or choose not to. Own your decisions. Be honest with yourself about why you choose or don't choose to do something.

- **Admit when You Don't Want to:** Instead of telling yourself that you're trying when you aren't, instead admit that you don't want to do something. This will either help you realize that you can still choose to get the task done, or help you come up with a plan for a better time to do it. Be real with yourself so you can perfect your sense of self-discipline.

Chapter 5: Avoiding Burnout and Overcoming Resistance

The Pareto principle, also known as the 80/20 rule is very effective for better time management. This principle states that 80 percent of your results in life are going to come from 20 percent of the actions you take. This realization will help you change your process of setting and achieving goals. This principle was named after Vilfredo Pareto in the year 1895 when he noticed there were about 20 percent of people who succeeded, while the rest fell into the bottom 80 percent.

He soon realized that almost all activity in economics also adhered to this pattern. 20 percent of people controlled 80 percent of wealth in Italy then. And this principle can be applied to many different situations for us today. You can use this to prioritize your days and tasks and become more productive and disciplined with your goals. So how exactly does the principle work? If you make a list of 10 items you need to get done, two items on the list are more important than the remaining 8 items. But the sad truth is that many people put off the top 20 percent of task items that matter the most, focusing instead on the other 8 items that don't matter much and won't bring them real success.

Using the Pareto Principle for Goals

You can use this principle for more effective goal-setting and to enhance your discipline. Follow these simple rules and you will be successfully applying the 80/20 principle and thriving as a result.

- **Make a List:** Begin by writing your 10 most important goals of the moment. Then figure out which one of them you would choose if you had to select the goal that will have the biggest payoff in your current situation. Place a number 1 next to that task. Next, choose the follow-up goal in terms of importance. You will soon realize that once you've completed this exercise that you've identified the 20 percent that will be most worthwhile. Focus on those before the others. Here are some more steps to help you along the way.

- **Tackle the Hardest Goal First:** The world is full of people who look like they're always busy but who hardly get anything done. That's because they are usually busying themselves with tasks that aren't very important, putting off the harder and more important goals. The valuable activities are usually the harder ones, but they will lead to a greater payoff. Just tackle the bigger goals first and the rest of your day will be a breeze. Resist the urge to do the easier tasks first.

- **Keep Your Eyes Ahead:** Although it's good to break your goals into smaller and more manageable tasks, you should have one major goal that keeps you motivated and disciplined to continue. This will be your fuel for the days that you'd rather lie around and be lazy. If your goal is to become the top CEO of your company, print out a photo of a successful businessman that you will look at every day. This can represent your vision of success. If you want to move into your dream home within five years, set your phone background as a picture of a similar house. These tricks will help you keep your major goal in mind at all times, even when the going gets tough.

Tips for Preventing Burnout

Although self-discipline sounds like being tough on yourself, it also involves knowing when to take a break. Without them, you will eventually burn out. Burnout gets in the way of your ability to think clearly and creatively, making you think in more rigid ways. This is what happens when you work overtime every single week and don't make time for relaxation or de-stressing. Here are some tips you can follow to prevent burnout, so you can stay on task with your goals.

Make Time for Creativity

What is your favorite creative activity? It could be singing, painting, or dancing. Whatever it is, make some time for it and don't neglect the enjoyment of the activity because you believe it isn't productive. Even when you can't apply that creative skill to your professional life, this outlet will help you de-stress and recover from your workload, keeping you motivated and engaged.

Get Up Often

If you, like so many other modern-day people, sit at a desk all day, you need to make sure you're standing up and moving around often. Most people stay sitting at their desks even when they're on break, operating under the illusion that the more immersed in their work they are, the better off they'll be. But the truth is that you aren't a machine and you need a break. Our bodies are built to move around, not sit sedentary all day. Try to stand up and stretch or take a quick walk around the office at least once an hour, but even more than that is better if you can.

Don't Avoid Others

Support is important for human beings, and more and more of them have no one to confide in about their personal issues, according to research. It's true that the more stressed out or exhausted we fell, the more we want to be alone, oftentimes. But the fact is that that is the last thing you should do in that situation. Make time for social interaction, even when you don't feel like it. You will be surprised at how big of a difference it makes in how you feel.

Kill the People-Pleaser

But just as important as it is to make time for social interaction with other people, it's equally crucial to make sure we're listening to our own inner guidance instead of others when it matters the most. Many of us say "yes" to people at work or in our personal lives just because it's easier to avoid confrontation, even when we're exhausted and need some time to unwind alone. Notice when you do this and try to get rid of the habit of being a people-pleaser.

Be Solution-Oriented

We already dedicated a section in the book to the importance of positivity, and this is a somewhat related point. Positivity makes you more creative and resilient, enabling you to think in terms of solutions instead of avoidance. The more you tune into positivity when you're on the brink of burning out, the more you will learn how to relax and recognize when you need a break. If your main goal is being productive at work, it pays to remind yourself that you won't be very successful if you keep going until your positivity (and as a result, your creativity and innovative thinking) has completely run out. Take the time to rest and recharge your batteries.

<u>Overcoming Resistance</u>

People are afraid of change. We are creatures of habit and like to stay in our familiar routines and bubbles without being disturbed. In fact, this is so true that people often dislike when *others* change too, even if it has nothing to do with them. Do you struggle with sticking by your heart's desires because you're afraid of what others will say? The truth is that people like stability and homeostasis, and they want you to remain predictable. But is that a reason to throw away your values and settle for a life you don't really want?

When you change in real ways, it will force the people around you to change too because they'll have to find new ways to respond to your shifts. A lot of people don't like this and will resist it. They might try to talk you out of a new job or a new look and won't be interested in hearing your logical reasoning behind your choice. How can you handle these reactions, both from other people and yourself? Should you give up on changing and stay the same old predictable you? Absolutely not! Here are some preparations you can make to handle resistance better.

1. Know Your Reasons

When your mind (or mother) begins to give you reasons why you shouldn't try something new, have your main motivation in mind. Don't allow this truth to waver at all and keep your mind on it no matter what happens. Be ready to defend yourself, if necessary, but don't go picking a fight. When you know exactly why you're doing something, words to the contrary have no bearing on you. If you are confident in your choices, the opinions of others (or of your own insecure side) won't be able to change your mind.

2. Have a Comeback Ready

Plan out what you will say if someone tries to talk you out of something you've already decided on. This comeback could be funny, logical, or whatever feels right to you. Imagine that you're about to make a career change and pursue the job you really want, but that you're leaving your old career behind and want to tell your parents about it. Think of what the likeliest response will be to your news, ("But you've had that job for 10 years, it would be foolish to quit now!") and prepare what you will say ahead of time. Make it clear that you aren't looking to be talked out of your choice.

3. Make New Friends Who Get it

It can be hard to follow a specific path if you aren't surrounded by people who understand it. If you don't have any friends who can support your new goal, it may be time to seek out some new ones. Join a club that revolves around your interest, or even an internet forum where you can discuss it. Support is crucial. Instead of seeking out encouraging words from the people who don't approve of your new way of acting, save your updates for people who do.

4. Share Your Progress (When Asked)

Odds are, when you begin to show that sense of satisfaction and happiness from your new changes, the people in your life will want some of what you're having. If you can tell that someone wants more information on how you made your change, be there to offer insight and tips. Don't preach to them about it, but answer questions if they ask. Change doesn't happen overnight, but you can be a good resource for someone if they are interested in taking a similar path or pursuing their own goal.

5. Be Tough

There are going to be instances where this new path you've chosen feels lonely and difficult. But this has to be your motivation to continue. When you push through these hard times, you have a chance to make real, lasting changes. This is what real self-discipline is all about; staying on your path even when it isn't easy. It's what separates the amazing achievers from the average Joes. Make a list of all the reasons why you are going after whatever your specific goal is. Any time you're struggling, review the list so you can remind yourself why you're doing what you're doing.

6. Remember That It's a Process

Don't ever forget that success is not just a single step, but an ongoing process. As soon as you achieve what you wanted more than anything in one area, there will be something else worth going after before you know it. Success is a long, varied path that you must be truly dedicated to in order to succeed.

Now you have all the tools you need to succeed in life. If you stick to the steps in this book, you will experience a total, radical shift in your self-discipline. With this information, you can become as fit as you want, find a new career, or build a beautiful relationship with your partner. You can apply these basic principles to your life no matter what your goal is.

Chapter 6 Final Thoughts

Thanks for picking up *Self-Discipline and Mental Toughness: A Guide to Developing Your Grit and Increasing Your Productivity*. I hope that this book gave you the inspiration you need to become a more self-disciplined individual and as a result, achieve your deepest dreams in life.

Life is full of problems and challenges along the path to achievement and success. But to get past these, you must be persistent, persevere, and develop a strong identity of self-discipline. This skill will give you healthy self-esteem, confidence in all you do, and satisfaction and general life happiness, as well. If you ignore or neglect to develop self-discipline, on the other hand, you could be looking at loss, failures, bad relationships, and low self-worth.

Whether your goal is to overcome a negative habit, improve your study habits, exercise more often, or rise to the top in your professional field, you need this skill. There are plenty of books out there on the market about self-discipline, so thank you for choosing this one. If you found it helpful, please take the time to leave it a review on Amazon! Thanks again and good luck out there.

Furthermore, the transmission, duplication or reproduction of any of the following work, including precise information, will be considered an illegal act, irrespective whether it is done electronically or in print. The legality extends to creating a secondary or tertiary copy of the work or a recorded copy and is only allowed with express written consent of the Publisher. All additional rights are reserved.

The information in the following pages is broadly considered to be a truthful and accurate account of facts, and as such any inattention, use or misuse of the information in question by the reader will render any resulting actions solely under their purview. There are no scenarios in which the publisher or the original author of this work can be in any fashion deemed liable for any hardship or damages that may befall them after undertaking information described herein.

Additionally, the information found on the following pages is intended for informational purposes only and should thus be considered, universal. As befitting its nature, the information presented is without assurance regarding its continued validity or interim quality. Trademarks that mentioned are done without written consent and can in no way be considered an endorsement from the trademark holder.

Declutter Your Mind

How to Clear Your Mind and Keep
Yourself from Getting Overwhelmed,
Exhausted and Stressed

By Martin Brandt

Contents

Introduction

Congratulations on downloading your personal copy of *Declutter Your Mind: How to Clear Your Mind and Keep Yourself from Getting Overwhelmed, Exhausted and Stressed*. Thank you for doing so.

The following chapters will discuss some of the many ways our mind can get cluttered. Between work and family stress, it is easy to get bogged down in the day to day grind, leaving little energy left for enjoying the day.

You will discover how important it is to streamline your day to avoid unnecessary mental clutter. Doing so will help you live your best life in a way that is stress-free.

The final chapter will explore some easy ways to maintain a decluttered mind for the long haul.

There are plenty of books on this subject on the market, thanks again for choosing this one! Every effort was made to ensure it is full of as much useful information as possible. Please enjoy!

Chapter 1: What Causes Mental Clutter?

Mental clutter is an easy phrase to describe the vastness of your thoughts, memories, and experiences. Every aspect of your daily life gets stored in your brain, and in such a small space, there is bound to be clutter. While it isn't known exactly why or how we can remember so many things. What we do know is that there is certainly a capacity at which we overload ourselves, and our overall function suffers from it.

Mental clutter is often synonymous with emotional baggage. We often let episodes from our past give weight and value to our present. For example, if you failed an important task at work, and you let it define you, an air of doubt is cast over your current work and ability.

Carrying on poor relationships is a big driver of mental clutter. Ideally, we would all like to say that we are in supportive, coexisting relationships. In reality, we all have relationships that are emotionally draining, at best. Think of that friend who always needs something, or always has something heavy weighing on them. Doesn't some of that negativity get transferred to you?

Is your home or work situation conducive to great emotions? Is your partner in crime really dedicated to you, or is the relationship forced? We often settle for relationships that are less than supportive for the sake of not being alone. At work, you may be surrounded by people that really want to see you fail, even if they seem supportive on the surface.

It is important to recognize these flaws in relationships so you may avoid the obvious pitfalls. It will always be necessary to carry on relationships that don't exactly suit you, but the goal is to navigate them in a way that benefits you. There will always be a bit of negativity, but if you make the conscious decision to avoid it, your emotional conscience will be clear, and your degree of mental clutter will be low.

You have the right to avoid drama in your life. We all know one person in our lives who always have something bad going on, or gets caught up in anything and everything bad. Their sister is having a fight with her husband, and it is making them sad today. They need to make sure their grown kids are getting off to work, and their husband's sister in law's friend had a death in the family, and suddenly get wrapped up in that. The downward spiral that ensues is inevitable. If you don't feel you know someone like that, take a look at yourself. This is probably you!

Leaning to this drama is against your better judgment, and you know it. The trick is separating yourself from situations that bring you down. Yes, it is conducive to a good friend to be there for friends when bad things are happening. It is another situation entirely to engross yourself and get caught up in that negative energy. Often times, you are only fueling that negativity when you choose to be part of it.

Very simply, mental clutter is anything that gets in the way of your focus at any given moment. That is, if you are thinking of other things, you are not wholly focused on whatever is going on in the here and now. This can certainly be emotional, as described above, but can be very simple things in life that bog you down as well. This can manifest itself in a number of ways.

We often see multitasking as a great thing, a real talking point on your resume. Being able to juggle many things at once is a valuable skill sought by most employers. This has also become insidious in our daily life. The ability to work, care for a family, make dinner and have a side hustle is considered a norm these days.

The reality is, if your mind is forced to focus attention on all of these things at once, it is not giving its undivided attention to any one thing. This is a real jack-of-all-trades, master-of-none kind of moment. What are you really gaining from doing so many things if you aren't doing any of them as well as you could? Think of the potential you could harness if you could just focus on one thing. Wouldn't you really knock it out of the park if all your attention was dedicated to something?

Mental clutter manifests itself outside as well. Environmental clutter is both a symptom of mental clutter and a cause of it. That is, what you surround yourself with can affect your mood and your ability to think straight.

Consider the state of your home or office space for a moment? Is it conducive to clear thinking? Are your spaces clear of unneeded items, paperwork, and junk?

Does everything have a space? Are there things out of place? All of these things unwittingly tax the mind. Your brain likes order, and when things are out of place, the mind tries to make sense of it. The mind will begin to wander, thinking about the dishes in the sink, the sock on the floor, the laundry pile, and putting things away.

Meanwhile, really productive, happy, exciting thoughts are pushed to the corner because the brain is already exhausted. It is really difficult to brainstorm for your business or have a candid moment when your brain is otherwise preoccupied. Take a look at your surroundings and assess whether or not it looks like a blank slate for thought, or if it looks like a to-do list.

Mental clutter is unavoidable all the time, but with the help of the ideas interwoven in this book, it is possible to eliminate and avoid adding new clutter to your daily life. Good navigation will allow your mind to focus on the task at hand, and really tap in to what is important and valuable in your life. Allowing this action is conducive to living your best life.

Chapter 2: Impacts of a Cluttered Mind

A chronically cluttered mind will have a major impact on your life, physically, mentally and emotionally. You may not even realize the effect it is having until you release some of this clutter. Basically, you are not seeing the forest through the trees.

Let's take a look at the physical impact first. It is often hard to relate your physical health to your mental state. Modern medicine has trained us to avoid seeing how our mental state affects our physical body, and we assume that any physical ailments we have are stand-alone problems.

In reality, our brain and body are deeply interwoven. You cannot separate one from the other. A great example of this is stress. We often think of stress as a mental thing. We feel stress from work and from keeping a tight schedule in our households. This stress makes us tired and unfocused, but it also wreaks havoc on our bodies. Stress raises hormones like cortisol, which cause us to stress eat and gain weight. It raises our blood pressure and creates problems within the heart if left unchecked. It also affects our digestive system, creating problems like Irritable Bowel Syndrome (IBS) that are generally thought incurable by modern science.

Early physical symptoms of stress are largely ignored. Minor aches and pains can be explained away by sitting too long or sleeping on something wrong. In reality, stress creates an inflammatory response in the body which causes pain in joints and muscles. It is a physical manifestation of stress. It is a real thing, something that science is just beginning to pinpoint.

The inflammatory response caused by stress causes the immune system to respond. Every time we need to use our immune system to deal with this low-level inflammation, it is taking away resources used to protect the body from environmental threats like bacteria and viruses. Symptoms of stress can simply cause you to get sick more often.

As chronic stress continues, the immune system gets tired and weak. It begins to recognize similarities in harmful substances and body cells. Since it can't tell the difference, the immune system begins to attack healthy body cells, causing autoimmune diseases. This is the case in diseases like rheumatoid arthritis, multiple sclerosis and thyroid disorders like Hashimoto's. It has been scientifically proven that stress exacerbates symptoms of Lupus, another autoimmune disease. Stress is real, and it all stems from a cluttered mind.

It is difficult to grasp how mind clutter can affect the body physically, at least until science proves it. It is very easy to recognize how a cluttered mind affects us mentally, emotionally and spiritually, however.

Mental clutter keeps us from living in the here and now. When the mind is consumed thinking about problems and reliving old emotions, you are not present in the current moment. Have you ever pulled out of your driveway and pulled into the parking lot at work, only to realize you don't remember the trip? Your mind knows the way to work, basically puts the present on autopilot, and slips back into thought. Maybe you are still ruminating over that odd comment your spouse made or thinking of how your day is going to go today. Either way, you are too busy with these thoughts to focus on the present moment.

What is the harm in that? Neglecting to live in the moment means you will be missing out on the natural interactions that happen around you. On your ride in, you missed the colors of the sunrise in your rearview mirror, missed that cloud that looked like a bunny soaring high above you. You unwittingly cut someone off, putting another driver in a bad mood for the rest of the day. You are not present. You are not living your life.

The pressure of this life we live means that we are always waiting for the next moment to happen. We are not engaged in the now because we don't feel we have time to let it play out. Have you ever rushed a conversation with someone because you had things to do? Was it really that important that you could not focus on this person for just another thirty seconds? Did you stand there listening for that thirty seconds but didn't really hear them? What is the point?

How about technology? How often do you skip interacting with someone because you are on the phone, or scrolling through social media? Keep in mind that your inner spirit, the force that drives you, existed long before the invention of social media. It thrives on interaction with others, with movement and physical progress. It does not understand the draws of social media. You are killing your spirit by skipping out on interactions in real life in exchange for this pseudo-world we have built around ourselves. Do you really even know those "friends" you have on social media?

Living in this day and age makes us emotionally numb. Avoiding interactions at all costs means that we are not really using our emotional intelligence. Unless you are fully engrossed in how something makes you feel, you are not actually living. You are not seeing the subtle nuances of life that bring you happiness, joy and a reason to live. The small interactions and appreciation we have at any given moment are what life is all about, and we are missing it!

Take some time to really hear what someone is saying to you. Give your undivided attention and understand the world that is going on around you. Let the past be in the past, and let it go. Hold no grudges, don't let the past define you. And don't worry so much about the future. You don't know what it holds, so there is no sense trying to plan it to a tee. Nobody truly knows how much time they have left, so spending it planning a future you will not have is a true waste. Instead, be thankful and live in the here and now. It is the only thing that is actually real. Everything else is just a figment of your imagination.

Chapter 3: Finding Your Focus

The key to finding your focus is digging deep into yourself to find what it is you care about most. What are your innermost hopes, dreams, and values? This will not be a quick and easy project, but most likely, you already have some inkling as to what that is.

Many alternative practitioners, like healers and seers, believe in the mythical Third Eye. While invisible to the naked eye, the space just between your eyes in the center of your forehead is said to hold the key to unlocking our inner wisdom, from our divine selves, harnessing the power of the universe. While somewhat mystical, it actually corresponds with the very real, physically existent pineal gland. While all of its functions are yet to be discovered, it has been shown to be primarily responsible for sleep patterns and self-awareness.

For now, we can use the mystical concept as a means for getting in touch with our inner spirit, what holds the truth behind all of our deepest desires. Tapping into this potential will allow you to discover your most essential dreams and values. We all are given an idea of what we should stand for by following the lead of those around us. We are generally nice and law-abiding as our forefathers did, and that is the structure society gives us.

What sets us apart from others are the individual things we hold dear. Because the pull of society and work and family are so strong, it is very easy to ignore the cues and directives of our inner spirit. If you have ever felt your conscience nagging at you, you can recognize the influence of your inner spirit.

What are the benefits of letting your inner spirit take the reins and guide you? Trusting your instincts and following your passions will absolutely transform your life. In a physical sense, you will be doing things on a daily basis that bring you happiness and joy. On a spiritual plane, you are taking advantage of a whole new level of energy that will guide your life.

If you're thinking this all sounds a little far-fetched, you are probably not alone. How do you even get in touch with your inner spirit? We will discuss how to do this in a bit more detail later in this book, but let's take a look at some concrete examples for the power this has.

After you have found what you want to focus your life around, things will simply start coming together. When you are in a good flow of energy, everything seems to work out in a concerted effort. You don't really struggle with much, as you actually enjoy the new challenges that are entering your life. This can easily be explained in a work-career scenario. Let's look at Jessica's story:

Throughout her early twenties, Jessica took a job at her local pharmacy. After several years working minimum wage at a local deli, just next door to this pharmacy, the prospect of making just a dollar more per hour above her current rate excited her. This job brought her opportunities, although it wasn't really in her field of study. Jessica took these jobs part-time while she was a full-time student of nutrition.

For the next five years, Jessica worked up the ranks at this pharmacy, receiving small pay raises for each year she continued to work. In this time, she had graduated college and purchased a home with her husband. They started to build a life. Jessica was so afraid that she was going to lose everything, all of her work decisions from that moment forward were based on money.

When the pharmacy raises started to lose their luster, she looked for jobs in her studied field of nutrition. After finding a job of comparable salary in her field, she decided to take a higher-paying job working for a generator repair company. Obviously, against her true passion. Being deeply embedded in her financial situation, Jessica certainly did not see this.

The next couple of years were miserable. She worked at a job she hated just for the money, meanwhile daydreaming of counseling clients and giving nutrition advice, the reason she studied nutrition in the first place. Her degree fell short of the qualifications to become a registered dietitian, her original goal. She told herself that she didn't need to have this title to be happy and successful, and this got her by for some time.

Unfortunately, after years of unsettled, unhappy jobs, her conscience got the best of her. The subtle hints and signals that went largely unignored for a number of years had finally become signs and symptoms. She gained weight, developed health problems, she fought with her husband, pushed people away, dreaded going to work in the morning. These were not symptoms of a normal life, but of her inner spirit dying.

Then the opportunities started to present themselves. A contact from an old friend in her field. This became a job offer for more money, and a job she had dreamed of. From there, an opportunity to finish her degree and become a registered dietitian. Embedded in all of that was the opportunity to live with a clean, satisfied conscience. She was doing what she dreamed of most, living the life that completely jived with her inner self.

Guess what? The signs and symptoms disappeared. The negativity washed away. In that process, she learned that she needs to trust her intuition, those nagging negative thoughts that are meant to deter from walking the wrong path. Today, she uses that intuition to guide her practice. She works freelance as a dietitian, taking jobs that appeal to her, and truly deciding what to do based on how it feels. Even better? The financial worries she once had all seem to work themselves out. The fun jobs seem to pay well, and when one job ends, something inevitably comes up.

Focusing on the needs and wants of your inner self will transform your life. Find that focus and run with it and everything will work out the way it is supposed to. Also, keep an open mind as to what your life should look like. Our physical brains often have a good picture of what life should look like, but you will find that following your happiness and values is much more fruitful than the big house and white picket fence.

Chapter 4: Streamlining Your Obligations

A great way to reduce mental clutter is to limit your obligations to things that don't matter that much. For example, stressing over a school bake sale when your heart just isn't in the cause doesn't make much sense. Yes, you love your kids, but are you really helping them, or any of the kids with the hundred dollars raised? Could your time be better spent elsewhere?

There will always be things we don't want to do and have to do, but there are bigger reasons behind them. For example, while you may not like your job, you go because you need to pay the bills, so your family has somewhere to live. Crossing that line becomes working overtime and exhausting yourself so your kids can have the latest and greatest toys. There is a fine line between necessary and excessive.

Tapping into your inner desires and what really drives you is a great way to streamline your obligations. Take a look at each thing that you do on a daily, weekly and monthly basis and assess whether or not it suits your ultimate purpose. It's okay to be a little selfish here. Remember that self-care is crucial to being an active, beneficial person to others. If you feel that other people's wellness comes before yours, you are missing the point. This is your life, and if you are not happy, you're not doing it right!

Start by making a list of things that you are responsible for. Break them into different categories.

Physically write them in different columns. Put things like work under the essential category, a collection of things you need to do to keep a roof over your head and food on the table. This will include things like work, travel for work, grocery shopping, cooking, cleaning the house, and the like.

Look at the things you do less often, and figure out where they fit. Maybe you care for a family member in your spare time, or you drive the neighborhood kids to school every day as a favor to their parents. These are things that aren't necessary to life but are driven more by your morals and values.

Determine whether or not each activity fits in to your moral conscience, or if it has just become something that is expected from you. If you are doing more things because you feel you have to than out of an actual moral need to do them, it is time to look at these events. Could you split carpool with another neighbor to take some of the responsibility off your shoulders? Why does it all have to fall on you?

Next, assess how much time you spend on each of these tasks. Is the majority of your time doing things that are necessary, and only a little bit spent on self-care and fun? Yes, you will probably spend quite a bit of time at work, and financially, it probably doesn't make sense to up and leave your job.

However, is it possible to cut your work down? Maybe you volunteer for special projects at work to try and get ahead. Would that extra time be better utilized at home with your family? Off on an adventure? Can you delegate tasks to others so that responsibility for some things can be shared? Lots of people end up being a martyr for their cause because they feel obligated to do work themselves. All you gain is less time to do what you really want to do.

What you can do is decide how to create more balance between the need-to-dos and the want-to-dos. Striking a good balance means you are living your life responsibly, but also making the most out of the moments you don't need to be working.

That's the safe way to go, and you know it. However, the next step may derail that thought process altogether. Yes, you can fit more fun, excitement, and meaning into your hours off the clock, but if the negativity that ensues during your work hours outweighs even the greatest days off the clock, you have a problem. It is vital that you be honest with yourself in this process, and it may relate to more than just work. Are you best friends with your grade school bestie because you still love them, or has the relationship gone south? Do you raise your kids with your spouse because you want to, or because you feel obligated to?

It is and will be difficult to come to terms with some of the decisions you have made, and it is up to you to listen to your conscience for guidance here. Keep listening to those subtle cues your conscience gives you. Use this inner wisdom to guide the decisions, twists, and turns in your life.

Finally, don't be so nervous about the financial side of life. We often get so bogged down with being in the green that we forget there is much more to life than money. Yes, it can create stability by paying for a safe and warm home, food to feed the family, and even fund vacations and adventures. However, lots of people forgo these fun things because they are busy working to make that money. They don't have time to take these adventures.

Assessing your obligations can be a daunting process, something that doesn't need to be dealt with all at once. Take it a day at a time and simply try to find balance in that day. For example, if you know you are working eight hours, what can you do in the other eight hours you won't be spending sleeping? There is quite a bit of time to be utilized, and you can certainly balance the work with some fun.

Starting each day with a bit of self-reflection and meditation can help your day get off on the right foot. Just take a few minutes to ask yourself what you want out of this day. How can you incorporate things into your day to make that vision a reality? What can you do today that will bring you one step closer to the life you live in your dreams? Life is about small bits of progress, you don't have to uproot your entire life to be happy.

Chapter 5: Importance of Boundaries

Creating boundaries within your life is a great way to stay focused on your true passions. We often get off track when we try to do too many things, cater to people and do things that are against our inner conscience. By eliminating some of these responsibilities and delegating some to others, we are creating boundaries. This also eliminates some of the noise going on in your brain, leading to clearer thinking on the things that are most important.

There are a number of boundaries you can set. First, let's begin with the physical boundaries. This may pertain to things within your home, or in your office space. Perhaps you have a tendency to collect things or have trouble throwing things away. It will be inevitable that these tangible things will pile up, creating clutter in your space, and your mind.

Set a limit on how much stuff can sit on your counters, how much laundry can pile up, or how much work is on your desk. Make a plan to respect these boundaries by taking action when that boundary is about to be crossed. For example, when the dishes pile up on one side of the sink, do the dishes. Do not simply let them start piling up on the other side. Tending to a task like this takes it off your plate before it has a chance to clutter your mind. Ignoring it and adding it to your long to-do list only adds to your stress.

Ignoring boundaries like this can also hinder your social life. You may refrain from having friends over because your house isn't presentable, or you may miss out on a day hike because your house is so messy that it will take the whole day to clean it up. Respect the boundaries you set so you can live a more functional, clutter-free life.

As a species, humans are relatively selfish. It's fine to do things for yourself, and it is encouraged. However, we also have a tendency to do things for others as a means to be socially accepted, to keep jobs and to make others happy. This need to please often trumps the need to be happy and at peace with yourself.

Work is a good example. We often see actors in cinema portray a weak, pushover-type employee being run over by their bosses. They are asked to stay late at work, disregarding family obligations, and end up feeling downtrodden and exhausted. The end of the two-hour ordeal usually leads to this person standing up for themselves and going off to follow their passions. You never see this person simply take it. End scene.

The reality is, most people actually do just take the abuse and keep their heads down, for the sake of complacency. Stop doing that. You have not been put on this earth to be someone else's minion. If you don't feel well-respected and appreciated in any aspect of your life, say something. Sure, you may not have a job that you are in love with, but you deserve respect and fair treatment. You do not need to be taken advantage of just to get ahead. Get ahead to what? More of this?

Keep in mind that we often create these breaches in boundaries ourselves. If the boss says something needs to get done in overtime, and you constantly volunteer yourself to be a martyr for the team, that's on you. It is important that you create boundaries that you follow in such situations.

Set goals by saying you need to be done with work by a certain time (most days) so you can be home with your family for dinner. Don't go in on a Saturday if your work can wait until Monday. You do not need to be a work superhero. If you happen to love your job and consider it your true calling, it is vital to set these boundaries for yourself, so you don't get caught up and lose out on time with family and friends. It's all about balance!

Striking healthy boundaries with others is definitely a challenge as well. If you have let people cross the line in the past, it may be difficult to set boundaries now, but it is vital to your health and happiness. If a friend constantly cries on your shoulder and asks for help, you may feel obligated to always help. If this is emotionally draining on you, it is time to take a step back.

While it may not be easy, have an honest conversation about it. Explain how the relationship you currently have makes you feel, and what you would like out of it instead. Think about how your enabling is actually hindering your friend. Would they learn to better stand on their own two feet if you were to step back a bit?

This conversation may end in one of two ways. Either your friend (or whoever this is) will respect and understand where you are coming from, or they will get defensive. This defensive stance is really a sign of manipulation. If they say anything to make you feel guilty for thinking what you think, they are manipulating you. Keep in mind that long-term, this person probably doesn't have your best interests in mind, you were only their crutch. Understanding this makes it much easier to create a healthy boundary.

Setting boundaries with people can lead to certain people leaving your life. It may happen fast, or subtly over time, but listen to your inner wisdom and know that this is okay. Certain people come into your life to teach you something. Even a great relationship can come to an end if all of the benefits have been exhausted. Certainly, that doesn't mean using someone and discarding them of course, but things will come to a natural end if they need to. If you stop wasting time trying to foster a relationship that is now forced, you may find new relationships to kindle. This process is about growth. You may find that these old friends circle in and out of your life at different times, and that is okay.

Setting boundaries and sticking to them is a sign of self-respect. If you are uncomfortable with the way someone treats you, touches you, or any aspect of your relationship, you have the right to stick up for yourself. You are just as important as anyone else, so don't allow yourself to be walked all over for the sake of keeping the peace. Sometimes the peace isn't meant to be kept.

Chapter 6: Simplify Your Surroundings

So far, we have talked a lot about the emotional clutter that fills your mind. Lots of the advice has been about making shifts in your thinking and tapping into what you really want out of life. However, we have also make the connection between the state of your surroundings related to the state of your mind. It all really comes down to one thing: to simplify your life, you need to simplify your surroundings.

We live in a world of excess. We buy houses that are too big to store all of the extra belongings we have, none of which have any stock in our true happiness. We keep things because we think it makes us who we are. We collect clothes, way too many things to wear in any given week, we have several cars, though we can only drive one at a time. We have extra rooms in our home for the guests we never invite over. So many things, yet, so little happiness.

What we have done instead is extended ourselves in a way that makes us work more, so that we may keep what we have. A big house means a big mortgage, more money to maintain, and a need to work more for it. We need to live within our means so this type of stress, and brain clutter doesn't exist. You should not spend the day thinking and worrying about how you will pay your bills each month. Surely, this doesn't mean selling everything you own and living in a tiny house unless of course, that is your true calling!

Instead, we can at least simplify what we have. Maybe you should assess and decide whether downsizing would relieve some stress and free up some more time. A smaller mortgage means you don't have to work so much! Perhaps it isn't the money, but the time wasted throughout the day.

Take a minute to ponder your daily routine. Does it take forever to dress in the morning because your closet is a mess and there are too many options? Do you spend an exhaustive amount of time on the road because you took a job far from home? Is it worth your time to clean your home, or would it be easier to hire someone to do it for you?

Simplifying your to-do list lends more time to the important stuff. First, look at the things that can be fixed with simple organization. If you have too many clothes, organize your closet and get rid of things you don't wear. Put all of your socks together, and separate your winter and summer clothes to make more room.

If your morning routine isn't an easy start to your day, figure out how to fix it. Do everything in the bathroom at once before moving on. Shower, brush your hair and teeth before you leave the bathroom to avoid extra trips. Get your breakfast ready and prepare your lunch before leaving the kitchen. Streamline the process. Sticking to the same routine means you will become faster at it, and it will take less thought, leaving more time for important thinking. A good morning routine preps you for the day, instead of leaving you mentally drained before leaving the house.

When it comes to a home or workspace, the look and feel are vital. It is possible to arrange things in a way that are relaxing and inviting, or conducive to work, depending on the needs for the space. Utilizing good interior design techniques with the concepts of Feng Shui can ensure that the spaces you walk in to are at their most inviting.

Think about coming home to a cluttered mess of a house with mismatched furniture and colors. Does it make you feel like relaxing? How about a home that has neutral colors, clean lines, and minimal clutter? Looks like there is nothing left to do but relax!

As you organize your space, find a designated spot for everything you have in your home. The kitchen is a great example. If making dinner is a huge production because the pot you need is under another pot, packed with something else in your cabinet, it will be exhausting to even think about cooking. Eliminate things you don't use and be mindful of the space you have. Keep only what you have space for, and choose wisely.

This goes for every room of the house, and your office as well. If it takes just as much effort to gather what you need for a project as it does to do it, you likely have too many things! You should know where everything is and have easy access to it. Your daily tasks shouldn't be so difficult.

As you go about transforming your spaces, think about how you want it to function optimally, not about how it is now. If rearranging your furniture would mean easier access to certain things, go ahead and move stuff around. For example, if your filing cabinet is not close to your desk and you often need to get up to gather things, move it closer. Think about how many steps are taken to get across your home or office, and if things were arranged differently, could it save you time? Save that time and energy and go out for a leisurely walk instead!

Everyone will have different needs from different spaces, so it is important to discuss changes with others in your home or office. Come up with a solution that works for everyone to avoid any strained relationships. Perhaps moving that filing cabinet closer to you makes someone else's job more difficult. Come up with a good solution together.

Chapter 7: Simplify Your Work

Is it possible to get more done in a day? We all get the same twenty-four hours, so why does it seem like some people can do exponentially more? Some people are simply able to work smarter, not harder or longer. As we discussed in the last chapter, making some organizational changes to your office space may help streamline the process, but changing your mindset for work may do you one better.

Most of us process work as a means to run out the clock. If you are meant to work for eight hours a day, you figure out what you can do to make that time go by. This is the wrong way to think about it. Instead, ask yourself what are you capable of doing in that time? Raise your expectations of yourself, get more done, and get ahead without spending any more time.

Would you need to stay late at work if you crushed your daily to-do list, and had time to do the extra stuff your boss wanted done? Could you be insanely productive and still be home for dinner? This is all absolutely possible, and it's all a mind game.

First off, go in with a plan. At the end of each day, create a quick to-do list for the following morning. Get it all down on paper so that you may turn your brain off when your day is done. Do not look or think about that list again until the following morning. Be present and mindful in your life away from work if you are not in the office.

Going in fresh like this is vital. Plan to tackle that to-do list by noon. Instead of spreading out work to last the whole day, schedule different tasks in at different times. Perhaps that sales report has historically taken all day, but you procrastinated most of the time. Make a point to get it done in the hour it really takes. Focus all of your attention on that task until it is complete, without distraction. Regroup mid-day to eat, fuel up, and reassess the day. What's left on the to-do list, and what can you add for the afternoon? Five minutes left at the end of the day? Make that phone call you think can wait until tomorrow. What else can you knock off the list? We sprint to the finish, not slow as we see it coming into sight.

Scheduling is key. Schedule certain times to address emails and take phone calls. You don't need to check your email every time something new comes in. It is acting as a distraction to the task at hand, and every time you divert your attention, even for a minute, it takes another few minutes to refocus your attention on your task. Shut off pop-ups and reminders, silence your phone, and only address what you need to at any given time.

Perhaps the way you go about tasks needs to be addressed as well. Are you doing things the fastest and easiest way? Could you get more done if you simply streamlined your process? Would it be beneficial to outsource some of your work to someone else, so that you can focus on the real problems? Maybe you spend a good chunk of time scheduling clients at your office. Are there programs that could ease this process? Would hiring someone makes sense? Delegating works especially well if you push things you don't like to do, or aren't good at to someone who does like doing those things. Work together with your peers to help streamline everyone's work. Everybody wins.

Keep an open mind to how you do things. Before the invention of computers and the internet, people would keep records on paper, and for most businesses, would be a time-consuming process. Instead of living in the stone age, people adapted to use technology to take some of the workloads. This leaves time and energy for more important things and gives you the ability to get more done.

This situation is ideal for those who own their own businesses. These people are not punching the clock, they are getting work done. If necessary, they pull long shifts and work through the night to see their business succeed. These people don't pussyfoot around because they are not getting paid for every hour they put in. Procrastinating does not improve the bottom line. Working nine to five and getting an hour's worth of work done does not improve the business or bring in money.

No matter what type of business you are in, working for yourself or someone else, the same attitude will be beneficial. If you need to spend time at work, go ahead and get as much out of it as humanly possible. It is your time, you might as well feel productive, energetic and happy doing it. Hard work is always rewarded. Go above and beyond, leaving it all on the table each and every day. If you do work for yourself, get eight hours-worth of work done in five and enjoy the rest of your day as you see fit.

Is it possible to feel inspired to get after it every single day, day in and day out? Yes! Creating a positive work environment will mean you like going to work, interacting with your peers, and having a physical space that is conducive to work. Set up your space, so it is organized and easily worked in. Keep extra files out of sight and out of mind. Keep only what you are working on out on your desk.

Surround yourself with reminders of why you work so hard to get through those tough moments. If you work to keep your kids in a safe and happy home, be reminded of that by keeping their pictures close. If you work for yourself, have images or quotes that signify this dream at the ready. It is easy to get bogged down in the details, so it is important to constantly remind yourself why you are doing what you are doing. Consider this part of the interior design.

Last, but not least, work with your natural energy. If you tend to be a morning person, put the tough stuff on the list for a time you will be fresh. For example, if prospecting for new clients takes a lot out of you, get it done first thing when you are at your best. When you are a little drained, do some mindless work, like filing or answering emails for a little quiet time. Some of the best minds out there get up and start work insanely early, as this is when they are at their mental best. Play to your strengths.

Chapter 8: Rid Yourself of Distractions

Attaining good mental focus and working with a decluttered mind requires ridding yourself of distractions. These production killers come in all shapes and forms, and each of us individually is the cause of our decreased productivity.

First, we need to get our mind right. Without that, the rest of the suggestions within this chapter are basically useless. Before beginning any task, you need to clear your mind of all other thoughts, so that you may focus only on the task at hand. We often get distracted thinking about things in our past and in our future, which are largely distracting to what is really important: the present. While multitasking appears advantageous to most, the reality is, if you are not concentrating on the task at hand, you are not doing it to the best of your abilities.

Come up with a mental process before sitting down to do anything. This may include some physical things too, which we will discuss later in this chapter. For example, you may decide that the tasks that involve quite a bit of concentration should happen after you have checked email, voicemail and anything else that might be intriguing your mind. Knowing that nobody needs anything pressing out of you helps ease the mind.

Depending on the task at hand, make sure you have gathered all of the tools, paperwork or information you may need before beginning. Having to stop and find what you are looking for disrupts your flow and jumbles the mind. For example, if you are cleaning the bathroom, make sure you have your cleaners and sponges ready to go before even stepping foot in there. If you are filing taxes, gather all of your paperwork and a calculator. Try to anticipate what you need so that the task does not become so stressful.

Next, take just a minute to create a game plan for tackling said project before you begin. Starting anything without a plan is a recipe for going off on a tangent, both in your mind and with the course of the project as well. Think about what you would like the outcome to be, and the basic steps for how to get there. For example, if you are creating an ad to go in your local newspaper, think about a few things it should get across, what color scheme you need to work with and how big the ad will be. Once that's down, you have a great template to work with.

If writing is more your style, making a quick outline to gather your thoughts is basically the same thing. Any big project may seem daunting until you create the outline and tackle it one section at a time. For example, outline each of your chapters, briefly describing its direction.

This intense moment of concentration requires all of your attention, so once this small action is done, your brain is already primed to take action. Run with that focus and try not to stop until you are finished or out of ideas. Let the flow run its course. If you stop to take a break, look at email, or anything else, you will need to get yourself back on track.

Distractions come in all places, not just in a working environment. We often become distracted by things that keep us from developing relationships, enjoying our time and living our lives. It is sad to think that we spend most of our time at work, and when we are not, we find ways to distract ourselves from having a life.

Social media and television are two of the most detrimental distractions out there. A few minutes quickly becomes hours of downtime, in which your brain has largely been shut off. While it is a good thing to let your brain rest, the addictive nature of these things really does hinder any progress in your work, personal and social life. The fact that meeting people and dating is now largely up to technology really proves how far this has gone.

Not only are these vices distracting, but they are also the cause of information overload. Our minds are not meant to take in such abundance of information all at once. It is more used to taking in the scenery of our environment and what is happening directly around us. Instead, we are getting news from all over the world, causing our mind to be in too many places at once. All of this noise is just adding detriment to your mental well-being.

How much time do you spend scrolling through social media or watching television? Do you truly get any joy or pleasure out of either of these activities or is it more to pass the time? The time you are passing is your life, which you are watching other people live on social media and TV. Why not put the phone down, get outside, and do something in real life? Instead of looking at social media, make a point to do something every day that you feel is worthy of sharing on social media.

Limit your time doing these activities and replace them instead with other things that are more valuable, things that improve your life, your health, and your education. Read a book, get out for a walk, get coffee with a friend. Switching up your downtime activities leads to a more satisfying, enriched life, and that is great for keeping your mind healthy and active. Plus, relieving stress with physical activities decreases mind clutter and improves all aspects of your life.

Everyone will have a different set of distractions. Take some time to pinpoint some of the big things that decrease your productivity, tax your brain and tire you out and do something about it. There is likely a

workaround to any distraction that exists, so
brainstorm some ways to make things run smoother.
Taking the time to address these problems now will
save you time and energy in the future.

Chapter 9: Recognizing Unhealthy Relationships

Now that we know how to work better, identify distractions and otherwise live an uncluttered life, it is time to assess some of the relationships you are involved in on a daily basis.

We are constantly surrounded by influencing people, and it is really up to you who you associate with. Some might say that you can't always pick who you work with or who your family is, but you can certainly choose how to carry out those relationships.

This is a tough chapter because it will force you to come to terms with the bad relationships in your life.

We all have at least one relationship that's a little dysfunctional, and that's okay. Nobody is the same, and it is common to butt heads with people.

However, there is a difference between normal disagreements and moral differences of opinion. It is these relationships that you need to be leery of, as they will prove to be mentally and emotionally draining over time if they aren't already.

There are a number of examples of bad relationships, but in general, if you simply have a hard time getting along with someone, seeing eye to eye on very little, you should probably limit contact with this person. It is certainly possible to have healthy disagreements and even heated arguments, but if there is not a level of respect on both sides, it may be best to part ways.

On the other hand, it is important to learn how to talk to frustrating people so that you can carry on necessary tasks, like working in the same office. You cannot simply find a new job every time someone rubs you the wrong way. What we're talking about here is irreconcilable differences. For example, if you can't stand how your boss runs their business, and it bothers you morally, there's no fixing that. But if you simply don't like the type of paper they order, get over it.

Personal relationships are the trickiest of all. Finding a partner or spouse is no easy feat. It takes a great deal of natural compatibility and sometimes downright luck to find someone to share your life with. The same goes for best friends as well. While you may not marry them, they will still be a big part of your life.

People you have in your closest circle should have your best interests in mind. If you constantly find yourself settling or compromising on things that you have strong opinions about for the sake of this other person, your relationship may be one-sided. Yes, good rapport with another person means compromising sometimes, but if your partner always gets their way at your expense, that's manipulation.

To go one step further, make sure you are not in an abusive relationship. If being with someone brings you down, makes you feel bad about yourself, or is physically or otherwise mentally abusive, you are not doing yourself any favors. The mental clutter that this person is causing inside your head is unreal. Your inner self, your spiritual conscience is wise and knows the outcome of your true path. If your conscience and your outside relationships are at odds, it will become very difficult to live your best life. The noise going on inside your brain to boot will become unbearable.

This isn't to say that less-than-desirable relationships cannot be mended, but remember that it takes understanding and commitment from both parties to make that work. If the person manipulating you is not willing to work on the relationship, it probably means that you are more invested in it than they are. More than likely, they don't know that how they are acting is affecting you in such a way, and coming to understand that helps to turn things around.

Have enough self-respect to know the difference. You need to know when to bite the bullet and cut ties with someone for the sake of your own mental health. Nothing is more important than fulfilling your innermost needs. Continuing to ignore them and go against the natural flow of energy from within you will only bring trouble and struggle for the rest of your life. Let in people that feel right, let others go that don't have your best interests at heart.

Let's turn it completely around for a second. It is absolutely vital for your growth and development to recognize if and when you are acting as the manipulator in a relationship. The concept of codependency is not a new issue. Partners, or at least one of them, often make each other feel guilty to get their partner to hang out with them. They pick fights and use guilt as a weapon to weaken and bring their partner down. This comes out of a lack of self-esteem and loneliness. If you can pinpoint when others are manipulating you, you need to take a hard look and recognize if you are doing this to someone else.

Not only are you harming this person you are supposed to love and respect, but you are also hurting yourself. Your deepest inner self wants none of that noise. It operates on love and light, not guilt and manipulation. Acting in such a way creates spiritual and mental clutter, as you are literally going against your own gut.

Relationships are fluent and can change moment to moment. It is important to recognize the difference between the natural ebb and flow of codependency, and understanding when it crosses a line. If you feel that you are being walked all over, the best thing to do is to express your feelings. Being true to yourself will take all of that drama out of your head and put it all out on the table. Once that's out there, let your partner decide if they are willing to work on it, or if they would rather not be such a big part of your life. As they say, if you love something let it go. If it's meant to be, it will come back to you.

Chapter 10: Mind Maintenance

Once you have freed your mind from the noise that tends to build up there, it is important to maintain it. Think of your brain as you would your muscles. You don't just build them and keep them, you need to continuously work to maintain them.

There are lots of little ways to maintain a clutter-free mind. The first thing is to avoid accumulating more clutter. Just as you would eliminate physical things that pile up in your home, you need to keep tabs on how you are feeling mentally, physically and spiritual at all times to avoid ending up right back where you started.

Remember that feeling tired despite good sleep habits is an early sign that your mind is cluttered. You are likely not sleeping as well as you think, and what brainpower you do have during the day is preoccupied with thoughts that don't serve you.

Do yourself a favor and take some time to check in with your thoughts every day. Are you feeling energized and clear? Is your brain foggy and sluggish? Do you feel anxious, angry or sad? Assess where you are so you can spend some time making improvements when necessary.

A great way to get in touch with your inner spirit and check in with your thoughts is to meditate. Taking just ten or fifteen minutes every day to sit and be inside your mind is a great practice. Meditation can be very simple and doesn't need to cut into your day. Set your alarm clock a few minutes early and take that time to lay in bed and simply think. If you feel you might fall asleep, physically sit up in bed, or try at another time of day.

Focus on the sound of your breath, or invest in a guided meditation soundtrack. The goal is to quickly get in touch with your inner self so that it can guide you. We all have an inner voice that helps us plan our day and our lives, but very few of us actually listen.

Some people say that exercise is a form of meditation, and to each their own. It is scientifically proven that exercise of all types helps reduce stress hormones, calm nerves and promote emotional well-being. Of course, it also strengthens the body and immune system as well, leading to better overall health.

Something as simple as taking a walk outside every day is enough to help clear your mind and get you thinking optimally again. If you tend to get inside your head when you are exercising, try using the activity as a dual meditation session. That is, concentrate and focus only on what you are doing. If you are out walking in the woods, take in the scenery and try to let other thoughts float to the back burner.

No matter the activity, it is important to give your mind time to rest and recover. Your brain is a sensitive organ, just like any other. It needs downtime to restore proper function. We can see the truth in this by recognizing how sluggish and foggy we are when we are running on little sleep. Downtime while awake is just as vital. Think of this downtime as an opportunity for the tiny librarians in your brain to sort through all of the open books and put them back on the shelves. Having this time to gather your thoughts makes you better able to make sense of them later.

People who are overworked often slip into their performance because they work TOO much. Yes, there is such a thing, despite what some of the world's most eccentric billionaires tell you. Taking breaks and allowing for rest actually makes you a better worker, allows you to be more alert and active in your daily life, and more proactive for your future.

On that note, keeping the past in the past and the future in the future is also vital to preventing the buildup of mental clutter. The most important moment in life is the one you are living right now. The rest is history, and we cannot predict what will happen in the future. There is no sense in worrying about things we do not yet know, and worrying means you are only suffering a second time provided that it actually comes to fruition.

Instead, take a mindful stance, and concentrate on being present and active at the moment. Focus on the work that you are doing, appreciate that you are hanging out with family and friends, and do things that strike your fancy at the moment. Learn to appreciate the subtle intricacies that are life, and soak in every moment. You truly don't know when your time is up. Do you really want to go out thinking about that horrible meeting you had yesterday?

A good rule of thumb is to check in with yourself at least three times during the day. Ask yourself a few good questions: Do you remember the ins and outs of what you have done over the past few hours? Do you feel as if you have accomplished something? Do you feel content? Excited? Agitated? Truly take stock of that time and decide where to fit in some balance. If you worked hard the last few hours, maybe it's time to give your brain a quick break and do something fun and silly for a few minutes.

What can you do in the next few hours to improve yourself? Find a shred of happiness and joy? Something that will propel you into the future you have always dreamed of? You must always keep thoughts of your innermost desires close to the front of your brain. Think of them as your operating manual. Are you acting in such a way that is in line with your innermost needs and morals? What can you do to better live those dreams?

Remember that mental clutter will dissipate more and more as you get closer to living your true inner passions and dreams. The energy of the universe will flow in your favor if you just give in to what your inner self truly desires. It's what YOU want, so why are you fighting it?

Final Thoughts

Thank you for making it through to the end of *Declutter Your Mind: How To Clear Your Mind and Keep Yourself From Getting Overwhelmed, Exhausted and Stressed*. Let's hope it was informative and able to provide you with all of the tools you need to achieve your goals of living a simpler, more meaningful life.

The next step is to organize your thoughts, develop a plan of action and start living your best life. In a few short weeks, you will be well on your way to living a clear, self-motivated life. Don't let the things that you enjoy pass you by! Finally, if you found this book useful in any way, a review on Amazon is always appreciated!

Furthermore, the transmission, duplication or reproduction of any of the following work, including precise information, will be considered an illegal act, irrespective whether it is done electronically or in print. The legality extends to creating a secondary or tertiary copy of the work or a recorded copy and is only allowed with express written consent of the Publisher. All additional rights are reserved.

The information in the following pages is broadly considered to be a truthful and accurate account of facts, and as such any inattention, use or misuse of the information in question by the reader will render any resulting actions solely under their purview. There are no scenarios in which the publisher or the original author of this work can be in any fashion deemed liable for any hardship or damages that may befall them after undertaking information described herein.

Additionally, the information found on the following pages is intended for informational purposes only and should thus be considered, universal. As befitting its nature, the information presented is without assurance regarding its continued validity or interim quality. Trademarks that mentioned are done without written consent and can in no way be considered an endorsement from the trademark holder.